YOU'VE SAT SPELLBOUND THROUGH MOVIE AFTER MOVIE— BUT HOW MUCH DO YOU REALLY REMEMBER?

STAR WARS: How many tie-fighters does Luke shoot down during the group's escape from the *Death Star*?

What specific type of robot is R2-D2?

FORBIDDEN PLANET: This film is considered to be an updated version of what famous play by Shakespeare?

THE DAY THE EARTH STOOD STILL: What is the final "message" Klaatu delivers to the congregation of Earth scientists?

BUCK ROGERS: Name three weapons in the arsenal of the leader of the good forces.

THE MAN WHO FELL TO EARTH: Who is the first Earthman that Newton encounters?

These are just a few of the brain teasers in this fantastic new collection of science fiction trivia. It's a stellar journey through your memories that you won't want to miss!

FROM THE BLOB TO STAR WARS: The Science Fiction Movie Quiz Book

SIGNET Books of Interest

FROM
THE BLOB
TO
STAR WARS:
The Science Fiction Movie Quiz Book

1001 Trivia Teasers for Sci-Fi Fans

By
Bart Andrews
with
Howard Davenport

A SIGNET BOOK
NEW AMERICAN LIBRARY
TIMES MIRROR

For My Friend Red

NAL BOOKS ARE ALSO AVAILABLE AT DISCOUNTS IN BULK QUANTITY
FOR INDUSTRIAL OR SALES-PROMOTIONAL USE. FOR DETAILS, WRITE TO
PREMIUM MARKETING DIVISION, NEW AMERICAN LIBRARY, INC.,
1301 AVENUE OF THE AMERICAS, NEW YORK, NEW YORK 10019.

COPYRIGHT © 1977 BY BART ANDREWS

SIGNET TRADEMARK REG. U.S. PAT. OFF. AND FOREIGN COUNTRIES
REGISTERED TRADEMARK——MARCA REGISTRADA
HECHO EN CHICAGO, U.S.A.

SIGNET, SIGNET CLASSICS, MENTOR, PLUME AND MERIDIAN BOOKS
are published by The New American Library, Inc.,
1301 Avenue of the Americas, New York, New York 10019

FIRST SIGNET PRINTING, NOVEMBER, 1977

1 2 3 4 5 6 7 8 9

PRINTED IN THE UNITED STATES OF AMERICA

Notes From Another World

This is my fifth trivia book. Little did I know, way back in 1966 when I discovered this fascinating "sport" at a Columbia University playoff, that I would someday become known as the "Maven of Trivia" (Los Angeles *Times*). Believe me, it isn't easy going through life—even in this galaxy—tagged an expert in trivialities.

Luckily, I found a few people, more or less sane, who share my enthusiasm for the obscure. When we get together, it's like a bonafide therapy session, only cheaper—though often just as humiliating! Our ranks continue to grow steadily, and it is heartwarming to receive letters from trivia buffs across the country. I love it! If you'd care to write, the address is Box 727, Hollywood, CA 90028.

Before I forget, the photographs in this book are from the Howard Frank Collection. They, and others, are available through Personality Photos, Inc., Box 50, Brooklyn, New York 11230.

Enjoy.

BART ANDREWS

Hollywood, California

P.S. I realize that the foregoing has little to do with the subject matter of this book, but the publisher pays by the word and I need a new car.

"STAR WARS" QUIZ

1. ROLE CALL

Match each actor with the role he played in *Star Wars*.

1. Chief Jawa
2. Chewbacca
3. Red Leader
4. See-Threepio (C-3PO)
5. Uncle Owen Lars
6. Gold Leader
7. Red Six (Porkins)
8. General Dodonna
9. Artoo-Detoo (R2-D2)
10. General Taggi

a. Anthony Daniels
b. Don Henderson
c. Alex McCrindle
d. Angus McInnis
e. Kenny Baker
f. Drewe Henley
g. Phil Brown
h. Peter Mayhew
i. Jack Purvis
j. William Hootkins

2. PLOT TEST

Arrange these ten *Star Wars* happenings in the proper chronological order.

a. Ben Kenobi convinces an Imperial trooper that he, Luke, and their companions are not the people the trooper is looking for.
b. Princess Leia places a gold medallion around Luke's neck.
c. The *Death Star* is destroyed by Luke.
d. Princess Leia's home planet is destroyed.
e. C-3PO loses an arm.
f. Luke's aunt and uncle are murdered by Imperial troops.
g. R2-D2 is programmed by the Princess.
h. Han Solo tries to convince Luke to join Chewbacca and him, instead of staying to fight with the rebels.
i. Chewbacca pretends to be a captured prisoner.
j. Luke, the Princess, Han Solo, and Chewbacca are trapped in a garbage hold.

3. WHO SAID THAT?

Who made the following statements to whom, and under what circumstances?

1. "He's got too much of his father in him."
2. "We don't serve their kind in here."
3. "Somebody get this big hairy walking carpet out of my way."
4. "I have the death sentence on me in twelve different systems."
5. "Was this trip really necessary?"
6. "Sorry about the mess."
7. "We seem to have been made to suffer."
8. "You came here in that wreck? You're braver than I thought."
9. "Who is more foolish? The fool, or the man who follows the fool?"
10. "Madness. This is madness. This time we'll be destroyed for sure."

4. LUKE SKYWALKER

1. How old is Luke?
2. What prompts him to convince his uncle to choose R2-D2 over the other robots?
3. What is the main conflict between Luke and his uncle?
4. When does Luke discover R2-D2's hidden message?
5. Who coaxes Luke into the *Millennium Falcon* after Ben Kenobi was cut down by Darth Vader's lightsaber?
6. When does Luke first use "The Force"?
7. How many tie-fighters does Luke shoot down during the group's escape from the *Death Star*?
8. How does Luke convince Han Solo to rescue the Princess?
9. When does Luke decide to join the rebel forces?
10. How is Luke saved from the Sandpeople?

5. BEN (OBI-WAN) KENOBI

1. According to Luke's uncle, what happened to Obi-Wan Kenobi?
2. How does Kenobi frighten off the Sandpeople?
3. What type of dwelling does Ben live in?
4. What does the Princess request of him?
5. What is his rank and title?
6. When and with whom did he serve?
7. How does his end in this "dimension" come about?
8. How long has it been since he used the name Obi-Wan?
9. What was his relationship to Luke's late father?
10. What is his warning to Darth Vader before the climax of their lightsaber duel?

6. PRINCESS LEIA ORGANA

1. What is the Princess's official title?
2. What is the rank and title of her father?
4. Whom does the Princess represent when she sends her message to Ben Kenobi?
4. What is her father's name?
5. What is her home planet?
6. She tells Moff Tarkin that the rebel base is located on_____.
7. What excuse did she use for her mission when questioned by Darth Vader?
8. In what cell is she held captive while aboard the *Death Star*?
9. How does she prevent the Imperial troops from reaching Luke and her on the catwalk?
10. Where is the Princess during the final battle?

7. HAN SOLO

1. Han Solo is a freighter pilot of what origin?
2. What is the name of his ship?
3. Where is it docked at Mos Eisley?
4. According to Solo, his ship "made the Kessel run in less than twelve standard_____."
5. How much is he to be paid for making the run to Alderaan?
6. To whom does he owe money?
7. What is the name of the alien he shoots in the cantina?
8. For what nefarious activity does Solo often use his spaceship?
9. How many Tie-fighters does he shoot down in the escape from the *Death Star*?
10. How does Solo save Luke during the final battle?

8. SEE-THREEPIO (C-3PO)

1. What talents do C-3PO possess that makes him desirable to Luke's uncle?
2. What is the robot's official function?
3. What does he fear will happen to him when Luke finds R2-D2 missing?
4. When does C-3PO try to convince Luke to abandon him?
5. Where is he during the final battle?
6. Which arm does he lose during the raid of the Sand-people?
7. How is he captured by the Jawas?
8. Where does he shut himself down?
9. What is he doing when Luke returns from the massacre of his aunt and uncle?
10. How does he get by the stormtrooper in the hangar control bay of the *Death Star?*

9. ARTOO-DETOO (R2-D2)

1. How many eyes does R2-D2 have?
2. What specific type of robot is he?
3. How does he trick Luke into removing the restraining bolt?
4. How many "feet" does he have?
5. What is his mission?
6. How tall is he?
7. What is R2-D2 designed for?
8. Where is he during the final battle?
9. What does Luke ask him to fix on the X-wing fighter?
10. How many Jawas carry him aboard their vehicle?

10. CHEWBACCA

1. What kind of "being" is he?
2. What color are his eyes?
3. What is he wearing when Luke first sees him?
4. What is his job aboard the Han Solo's spacefreighter?
5. What is his nickname?
6. From what cellblock does Luke claim Chewbacca is being transferred?
7. Why does Chewbacca become angry at R2-D2?
8. What is his reaction after the Princess hugs him when they escape the *Death Star*?
9. Where does Luke meet Chewbacca?
10. How old is he?

11. LORD DARTH VADER

1. What is Darth Vader's Imperial title?
2. As a young man, what was he trained to be?
3. Who was his mentor?
4. What color is his body armor?
5. What does he wear that no other stormtrooper wears?
6. What does he do when the captain of the Princess's vessel refuses to tell him his mission?
7. How does he "suffocate" General Taggi?
8. Why does he order Tie-fighters to pursue the rebels during the final battle?
9. How does he know the *Millennium Falcon* is carrying the tapes he is looking for?
10. Who is the first rebel fighter pilot he shoots down?

12. GRAND MOFF TARKIN

1. What is his official function?
2. What color is his uniform?
3. How many rows of ribbons does Tarkin wear on his tunic?
4. What ship does he command?
5. Why does he decide against "terminating" the Princess?
6. Who is his second in command?
7. What is his plan for extracting information out of the Princess?
8. Why does Tarkin decide to demonstrate the power of his ship against Alderaan?
9. Why does he allow the *Millennium Falcon* to escape?
10. Why does he refuse to leave his ship during the final battle?

13. WHAT IS IT?

Match the *Star Wars* paraphernalia with their descriptions.

1. Landspeeder
2. Councillor Vessel
3. X-wing
4. Skyhopper
5. Photon Torpedo
6. Gaderffii
7. Sandcrawler

8. Y-wing

9. Lifeboat Pod

10. Tie-fighter

a. Emergency escape vehicle
b. Rebel fighter craft
c. Jawa vehicle used for scavenging
d. Imperial fighter craft
e. Weapon used by Sandpeople
f. Light-duty transport vehicle
g. Weapon launched from fighter's craft
h. Galactic cruiser used for diplomatic missions
i. Tropospheric craft used on Tatooine
j. Rebel fighter craft

14. SPACE QUERIES

1. What color are the energy bolts fired from the hand-held blasters?
2. Where does Luke fix C-3PO's arm?
3. What gave the Jedi Knights their special power?
4. Han Solo prepares his ship for a _____ to go faster than the speed of light.
5. How tall are the Jawas?
6. What color is the liquid Luke drinks during the conversation with his aunt and uncle at dinner?
7. What protects the *Millennium Falcon* from the fire of pursuing destroyers?
8. What is the number of the garbage hold into which Luke and his companions fall?
9. According to Han Solo, how fast will the *Millennium Falcon* go?
10. What color is Darth Vader's lightsaber?

15. WHO . . .

1. . . . are the Jedi Knights?
2. . . . is General Motti?
3. . . . is Red Six (Porkins)?
4. . . . is General Taggi?
5. . . . is General Willard?
6. . . . is Beru Lars?
7. . . . is General Dodonna?
8. . . . was the original master of C-3PO and R2-D2?
9. . . . are the Tusken Raiders?
10. . . . warns Luke that the Sandpeople are coming?

16. WHAT . . .

1. . . . is Darth Vader looking for when he captures Princess Organa's star cruiser?
2. . . . is Anchorhead?
3. . . . are the names of the twin suns of Tatooine?
4. . . . color are the Jawas' eyes?
5. . . . does Ben Kenobi say to Luke after they evade the first group of stormtroopers at the spaceport?
6. . . . are Banthas?
7. . . . clue is found by the Imperial troops that leads them to search for R2-D2 and C-3PO?
8. . . . order did Luke's father belong to?
9. . . . is the call number of the Imperial troops who come to scan the *Millennium Falcon*?
10. . . . does C-3PO find at the top of the large dune shortly before he is captured?

17. WHEN . . .

1. . . . is C-3PO captured by the Jawas?
2. . . . did Luke's father die?
3. . . . does Owen Lars discover that Luke is missing?
4. . . . does Ben Kenobi present Luke with the lightsaber?
5. . . . are C-3PO and R2-D2 completely clean and shining?
6. . . . does the Princess kiss Luke for the first time?
7. . . . is R2-D2 knocked flat on his front?
8. . . . is Darth Vader *sure* that Ben Kenobi is aboard the *Death Star*?
9. . . . does Han Solo say "May the Force be with you" to Luke?
10. . . . is the *Death Star*-released information R2-D2 contains finally displayed?

18. WHERE . . .

1. . . . is C-3PO when R2-D2 is programmed by the Princess?
2. . . . does Owen Lars want C-3PO and R2-D2 to work on his farm?
3. . . . are C-3PO and R2-D2 reunited after they split up in the Tatooine desert?
4. . . . does Luke's search for R2-D2 lead him?
5. . . . is the spaceport on Tatooine located?
6. . . . does C-3PO fear he will be sent if the Imperial troops capture him?
7. . . . is Luke when R2-D2 makes his escape from the farm?
8. . . . does Luke claim he is from when the Imperial troops question him at the spaceport?
9. . . . is Han Solo when he is approached by Ben Kenobi with a job offer?
10. . . . are the rebel headquarters located?

19. WHY . . .

1. . . . does Darth Vader send his troops after the escape pod?
2. . . . does Owen Lars decide to acquire R2-D2?
3. . . . is Luke afraid to go after R2-D2 at night?
4. . . . does C-3PO think his friends have been crushed in the garbage hold?
5. . . . is C-3PO worried about R2-D2 after the final battle?
6. . . . does Luke forsake the use of his targeting computer?
7. . . . does Ben Kenobi become faint while training Luke with the lightsaber?
8. . . . doesn't Chewbacca want to escape through the hole blasted out by the Princess?
9. . . . does the tentacled monster in the garbage hold release Luke?
10. . . . is Han Solo afraid to make a hasty jump into hyper-space?

20. HOW . . .

1. . . . does Darth Vader hide the fact that he has destroyed the Princess's councillor vessel?
2. . . . did Luke's father die?
3. . . . does Luke raise the fee needed for their passage to Alderaan?
4. . . . does the *Death Star* capture the *Millennium Falcon*?
5. . . . does C-3PO save his friends who are trapped in the garbage hold?
6. . . . does Ben Kenobi know that the Jawas have not been ambushed by the Sandpeople?
7. . . . does the Emperor wipe out the remnants of the Old Republic?
8. . . . is the *Death Star* destroyed?
9. . . . does Luke know that the massacred Jawas are the same ones who sold his uncle the robots?
10. . . . did Luke find out that the Princess was on the *Death Star*?

21. BEHIND THE SCENES

Match the production personnel with their functions.

1. Gary Kurtz	a. Composer
2. Marcia Lucas	b. Makeup Supervisor
3. John Williams	c. Writer-Director
4. Gilbert Taylor	d. Director of Photography
5. John Molli	e. Production Designer
6. Stuart Freeborn	f. Chief Model Maker
7. John Barry	g. Producer
8. George Lucas	h. Costume Designer
9. Grant McCune	i. Co-Editor
10. Ralph McQuarrie	j. Planet and Satellite Artist

22. TRUE OR FALSE?

1. Luke receives the first medal awarded by the Princess.
2. Luke destroys Darth Vader in the final battle.
3. C-3PO likes Jawas.
4. Luke's brother has joined the Alliance.
5. Ben Kenobi is Luke's third cousin.
6. Han Solo winks at the Princess after she awards him his medal.
7. The rebel base is located on Yavin.
8. The truth serum used by Darth Vader's mind-probe forces the Princess to give up her secret.
9. General Willard is a member of the Rebel forces.
10. The *Death Star* destroys Tatooine.

23. GEORGE LUCAS

1. How old is Mr. Lucas?
2. How long did it take to produce *Star Wars*?
3. From what film school did he graduate?
4. What production position did he maintain on the film *The Rain People*?
5. What was his first commercially released film?
6. Where does he live?
7. What was his last film before *Star Wars*?
8. Whose work was the impetus for *Star Wars*?
9. What was the total budget, including the cost of publicity, of the film?
10. How many people were employed in the making of *Star Wars*?

24. YOU NAME IT!

Match the hardware used in *Star Wars* with their descriptions.

1. Vaporator
2. Lightsaber
3. Incom T-65
4. Tractor Beam
5. Hyperspace
6. Macrobinoculars
7. Repulsor
8. Fusioncutter
9. Remote
10. Energy bolt

a. A chrome orb used as a training device
b. Highly sensitive binoculars
c. Destructive energy released by hand-held weapons
d. Motivating power source for landspeeders
e. A weapon similar to a blaster but more powerful
f. A machine used to extract moisture on Tatooine
g. Ancient weapon of the Jedi Knights
h. A beam of pure energy which can hold objects in space
i. A skyhopper similar to an X-wing fighter
j. A distorted space-time continuum which allows faster-than-light travel

25. THE FINAL BATTLE

1. As the rebel fighters approach the *Death Star*, what do they encounter that causes their fighters to shake?
2. Who is Luke's squadron commander?
3. What is Luke's call number?
4. According to Luke, this mission is like _____.
5. When does Luke shoot down his first Tie-fighter?
6. Who is the first rebel pilot in Luke's squadron to be shot down?
7. Who shoots down the first Tie-fighter that is pursuing Luke?
8. How is the arrival of Darth Vader and his two cohorts reported?
9. Who fires the first salvo of photon torpedos?
10. Who makes the final torpedo run on the *Death Star*?

SCIENCE FICTION QUIZ

26. "METROPOLIS"

1. What is the robot's name?
2. Who directed this film?
3. In what year is the story set?
4. What was the total cost of the movie?
5. Who is the Master of Metropolis?
6. Who wrote the novel on which the film was based?
7. When, where, and by what company was the film produced?
8. Name the scientist who builds the robot.
9. How are the workers' homes destroyed?
10. Who was responsible for the cinematography?

27. NAME THAT MONSTER

Can you identify the movie monsters from these clues?

1. This monster lurks outside the dome in *Captain Nemo and the Underwater City*.
2. This long-dormant monster is revived to battle another monster.
3. Evil entities live inside metal mobile cones.
4. This monster's mother came looking for him when he was captured for exhibition.
5. This monster took over the mind of John Agar.
6. He came to Earth from Venus, and met his end in Rome.
7. This is a good-natured monster who has a turtle-like shape.
8. This monster accompanied alien teenagers to Earth.
9. He seeks to start a master race with an unwilling mate.
10. He came from Ganymede and his mission was to transmit girls to his home.

28. MOVIE MAKERS

Match the producer(s) with his film.

1. George Pal   a. *The Day the Earth Stood Still*
2. Julian Blaustein   b. *Destination Moon*
3. Walter Seltzer   c. *Them!*
4. Paul N. Lazarus III and
   James T. Aubrey   d. *Sleeper*
5. Saul David   e. *20,000 Leagues Under the Sea*
6. David Weisbart   f. *War of the Colossal Beast*
7. Walt Disney   g. *Visit to a Small Planet*
8. Charles H. Joffe and
   Jack Grossberg   h. *The Omega Man*
9. James H. Nicholson and
   Samuel Z. Arkoff   i. *Logan's Run*
10. Hal B. Wallis   j. *Futureworld*

29. "INVASION OF THE BODY SNATCHERS"

1. When was the film released, and by what company?
2. Name the director.
3. Who wrote the serialized novel on which the film was based?
4. In what town does the story take place?
5. Identify the male lead and the name of the character he played.
6. What character did Sam Peckinpah play?
7. Identify the female lead and the name of the character she portrayed.
8. Who did the music?
9. How many attempts were made to duplicate the protagonist by using a pod?
10. Who was responsible for special effects?

30. I WANT A RAYS

Here are clues to films that featured various types of rays. Can you identify the movies?

1. Ray Milland experiments with an eye serum, producing startling results.
2. Laurence Olivier becomes involved with an antiaircraft ray.
3. The Wizard's traffic-paralyzing ray is stopped by the Dynamic Duo.
4. A man is able to penetrate walls, but finds he must absorb other peoples' "life force."
5. Bela Lugosi slays his victims with a death ray.
6. James Bond is nearly dismembered by a destructive ray.
7. A paralyzing ray catches the people of Paris in various acts.
8. This destructive ray employs sunlight.
9. John Wayne encounters the perils of an antiaircraft ray.
10. A benevolent Gamma Ray is rewired to become a destructive Delta Ray.

31. SPACING OUT

Match the description with the movie.

1. Travelers destined for the moon go off course   a. *Project Moon Base*
2. A film adaptation of Jules Verne's classic   b. *Flight to Mars*
3. A hideous beast inhabits Mars   c. *Conquest of Space*
4. Rock creatures inhabit a well-known satellite   d. *It! The Terror from Beyond Space*
5. Giant reptiles inhabit an alien planet   e. *First Man into Space*
6. The U. S. beats Communists for control of moon   f. *From the Earth to the Moon*
7. An astronaut becomes encased in a metal crust   g. *Missile to the Moon*
8. A journey to the red planet   h. *Rocketship XM*
9. A monster creates havoc aboard spacecraft   i. *King Dinosaur*
10. The story of a first landing on Mars   j. *The Angry Red Planet*

32. "THEM!"

1. Identify the actors who played Sgt. Ben Peterson, Robert Graham, Crotty, and the Sergeant.
2. Who wrote the story upon which the film is based?
3. When and by whom was the film released?
4. Name the director.
5. Where is the last queen ant killed?
6. What caused the ants to become monstrous?
7. Where are the ants first found?
8. What character does John Weldon portray?
9. What is used to destroy the eggs?
10. From what does the picture take its title?

33. AHEAD OF ITS TIME

From these clues, can you identify films set in the future?

1. In this world of the future, people travel about in electric chairs.
2. Jean Renoir did this film, set in 2028.
3. New York in 1980.
4. Airship passengers pelt pedestrians with cabbages, and are pursued by police on aerocycles.
5. Books are forbidden in this future society.
6. A scientist steps out of a safe to discover a future time when women are the ruling class.
7. The plans for an impending attack are in the mind of a future-agent.
8. A nursery toy becomes a full-dimensional total experience.
9. The bombing of London by radio-controlled aircraft.
10. This society is under the watchful eye of the Thought Police.

34. OSCAR WINNERS

Match the movie with the award or awards it won.

1. *Destination Moon*
2. *When Worlds Collide*
3. *War of the Worlds*
4. *20,000 Leagues Under the Sea*
5. *The Time Machine*
6. *Fantastic Voyage*
7. *Dr. Jekyll and Mr. Hyde*
8. *2001: A Space Odyssey*
9. *Charly*

a. Art Direction, 1954
b. Art Direction, 1966
c. Special Effects, 1960
d. Special Effects, 1951
e. Best Actor, 1931-32
f. Special Effects, 1950
g. Special Effects, 1968
h. Special Effects, 1954
i. Special Effects, 1953
j. Best Actor, 1968
k. Special Effects, 1966

35. "THE INCREDIBLE SHRINKING MAN"

1. With what does the diminutive man fight off the spider?
2. Who was the director?
3. When, and by what company was the film released?
4. What is Scott Carey's job?
5. What happens when a water heater bursts?
6. Name the screenwriter.
7. How does he die?
8. Who played Scott and Louise Carey?
9. How is he miniaturized?
10. What three men were responsible for the special photography and optical effects?

36. TRUE OR FALSE?

1. *The Omega Man* is based on the novel *I Am Legend* by Harlan Ellison.
2. In *Colossus: The Forbin Project*, American and Chinese super-computers link up to control the world.
3. Jerry Lewis was a Kreton in *Visit to a Small Planet*.
4. Robert Vaughn was a prehistoric teen in *Teenage Cavemen*.
5. The movie *Fire Maidens of Outer Space* featured Mary Tyler Moore in a minor role.
6. *The Son of Frankenstein* featured Boris Karloff, Bela Lugosi, Basil Rathbone, and Lon Chaney, Jr.
7. George Pal produced the 1950 hit, *Rocketship XM*.
8. The first *Godzilla* film was released in the United States in 1956.
9. The first version of *The Lost World* featured Wallace Beery.
10. *Destroy All Monsters* featured ten—count 'em, ten—monsters.

37. TIME TRAVEL

Match the film with its brief description.

1. *Atomic Man*

2. *The Time Machine*

3. *The Time Travelers*

4. *Dimension 5*

5. *Time Flies*

6. *Cyborg 2087*

7. *World Without End*

8. *The Three Stooges Meet Hercules*

9. *Terror from the Year 5,000*

10. *Beyond the Time Barrier*

a. A "timeball" takes a young boy to meet Good Queen Bess

b. Three well-known clowns meet a legendary giant

c. A man dons a time-conversion belt to save a city

d. During an operation, a man is put seven seconds ahead in time

e. A future-man returns to the past to halt mental telepathy experiments

f. A disfigured woman arrives via Dr. Erlings' Time Vault

g. On a trip to Mars, an astronaut is thrown into a time warp

h. This voyage begins in 1899

i. A hypersonic vehicle conveys a test pilot into the future

j. Preston Foster finds a dying world of Mutants and Androids

38. "FORBIDDEN PLANET"

1. This film is considered to be an updated version of what famous play by Shakespeare?
2. Name the director.
3. What is the name of the planet?
4. Who is Dr. Morbius's daughter?
5. What is the number and designation of the Earth ship?
6. What is the monster?
7. What was the super-race that left the remnants of their civilization on the planet?
8. What is the name of the robot?
9. Can you recall how much was spent on the production?
10. When and by what company was the film released?

39. FLASH GORDON

1. Who created the comic strip upon which this Universal serial was based?
2. List three *Flash Gordon* serials featuring Buster Crabbe.
3. Who directed the first series?
4. What is the name of the planet which is approaching Earth?
5. Who played Dale Arden in the first serial?
6. Name five of the menaces faced by Flash upon his departure from Earth.
7. Who is the ruler of the evil planet?
8. What is used to suck away the Earth's atmosphere in the first series of shorts?
9. Who is the ally of the ruler of the evil planet?
10. What menaces does Flash encounter on Mars?

40. THE FUTURE PAST

Match the film with the time in which it was set.

1. *Soylent Green*   a. 2072
2. *The Time Machine*   b. 40,000
3. *Forbidden Planet*   c. 2015
4. *Things to Come*   d. 2022
5. *Barbarella*   e. 802,701
6. *Captive Women*   f. 2020
7. *Beyond the Time Barrier*   g. 2036
8. *Silent Running*   h. 3000
9. *World Without End*   i. 2024
10. *Spaceflight IC-I*   j. 2508

41. "NIGHT OF THE LIVING DEAD"

1. How do the dead come back to life?
2. Who played Barbara and Johnny?
3. What happens to Judy when she escapes from the house?
4. When was the film released?
5. Who was the director?
6. When does Ben meet Barbara?
7. What is Ben's fate?
8. How many of the living dead are black?
9. Who wrote the screenplay?
10. Where is Johnny killed?

42. "PLANET OF THE APES"
—PART ONE

1. From which *Ape* film is the following quote taken and who said it: "I can't help thinking that somewhere in the Universe there has to be something better than man, . . . has to be"?
2. List all five *Ape* films in their exact order of release.
3. Which *Ape* film received two Academy Award nominations? Name the categories.
4. All five movies were released by what company?
5. Who directed the first *Ape* film?
6. Who produced the series?
7. Who were the co-authors of the first screenplay?
8. In the conclusion of *Beneath the Planet of the Apes,* who detonates the Doomsday bomb?
9. The author whose novel is the basis for the films wrote another book that became a huge cinema success. Name the book/film.
10. In which *Ape* films did Charlton Heston appear?

43. "PLANET OF THE APES" —PART TWO

1. Pierre Boulle wrote the treatment for the first sequel. Name it.
2. From what film school did the producer graduate?
3. In the final scene of *The Planet of the Apes*, what is half-buried in the sand?
4. Who composed the music for the first film?
5. Which of the original astronauts survives captivity in the first movie?
6. Who wrote the screenplays for the last four versions?
7. In which *Ape* film did James Franciscus appear?
8. Who played Dr. Zaius in the first two productions?
9. Which three apes escape destruction in the second version?
10. In which *Ape* films did Roddy McDowall appear?

44. "PLANET OF THE APES" —PART THREE

1. What is the name of Zira and Cornelius's baby in *Escape from the Planet of the Apes*?
2. Kim Hunter appeared in which three *Ape* movies?
3. Who plays the circus owner in *Escape from . . . ?*
4. Name the directors of the last four *Ape* films.
5. Claude Akins was what character in *Battle for . . . ?*
6. Who is the leader of the mutants in *Battle for . . . ?*
7. Why did Armando kill himself in *Conquest of . . . ?*
8. Who was the Lawgiver in *Battle for . . . ?*
9. How does Caesar's son die in *Battle for . . . ?*
10. In *Battle for the Planet of the Apes,* where does Caesar learn about his parents?

45. CHARACTER STUDY

Match the character with the actor who portrayed the role, and then name the film.

1. John Cable
2. Montag
3. Winston Smith
4. Flesh Gordon
5. Count Dakkar
6. Dr. Zarkov
7. Alita
8. Phineas T. Barnum
9. Donatas Banionis
10. Dr. Rynning

a. Raymond Massey
b. Frank Shannon
c. John Carradine
d. Edmond O'Brien
e. Lionel Barrymore
f. Chris Kelvin
g. Marguerite Chapman
h. Burl Ives
i. Oskar Werner
j. Jason Williams

46. "2001: A SPACE ODYSSEY"

1. What short story was the film based on, and who wrote it?
2. Why is a mission sent to Jupiter?
3. Who were the special effects supervisors?
4. What is the name of Bowman's crewmate?
5. The space shuttle belongs to what real-life company?
6. How many astronauts are in hibernation aboard the Jupiter probe?
7. Who provided the voice of Hal 9000?
8. What is the name of the Russian scientist encountered aboard the orbiting space station?
9. The "failure" of what piece of equipment causes Poole to go outside the ship?
10. Identify the composers whose works appear on the soundtrack.

47. "THE OUTER LIMITS"

Fill in the words missing from the opening dialogue of this 1960's television series.

There is —1— with your —2—; do not attempt to —3—. We are controlling —4—. . . . For the next hour sit quietly and we will —5— all that you —6— and —7—. You are about to —8—, you are about to —9— which reaches from the inner mind to the —10—.

48. "I MARRIED A MONSTER FROM OUTER SPACE"

1. To what are the invaders allergic?
2. What is the name of the dog that Marge gives to Bill?
3. Who produced and directed the film?
4. When was Bill taken over by the invaders?
5. What happens when Marge sends a telegram to the F.B.I.?
6. Who played Bill and Marge Farrell?
7. What is the first dead animal Marge discovers?
8. What character did Maxie Rosenbloom portray?
9. When does Marge suspect that something is wrong with her husband?
10. When and by what company was the film released?

49. AD ART

Here are the advertising slogans used to promote some sci-fi films. Can you identify them?

1. "What will the next 100 years bring to mankind?"
2. "Your blood will turn ice-cold!"
3. "Adventurers conquer space with first passenger-carrying rocket!"
4. "They'll love the very life out of your body!"
5. "Bloodless—that's why he wants yours!"
6. "Thank God it's only a motion picture ! ! !"
7. "Creeping, crawling, flesh-eating maggots!"
8. "Age transformed to youth! Monkey glands!"
9. "They came to conquer the world . . . so young . . . so innocent, so DEADLY!"
10. "Blood-curdling giant fly-creature runs amuck!"

50. YOU SAID IT!

In what films were these words spoken, and by whom?

1. "Labor Omnia Vincit!"
2. "Come, my Martian bride, to Earth and love and life!"
3. "With my Cavorite, we shall go to the moon!"
4. "Radio-activity will make me Emperor of the Universe, of the planets, of all Creation!"
5. "Now for the rule of the Airmen, and a new life for mankind!"
6. "By the grace of God, and in the name of the United States of America, I take possession of this planet!"
7. "We have made machines out of men; now we will make men out of machines!"
8. "I hardly know how to tell you, but we are completely off course. We are heading for Mars!"
9. "An intellectual carrot? The mind boggles!"
10. "After all man could do had failed, the Martians were destroyed by the littlest things that God in His wisdom had put on the Earth!"

51. "THE DAY THE EARTH STOOD STILL"

1. Under what circumstances was Klaatu shot soon after landing?
2. Who directed the film?
3. What is the name of Klaatu's robot?
4. When was the film released and by what company?
5. Name the author and the work upon which the film is based.
6. What is the gift Klaatu brings for the President?
7. In what city does Klaatu's ship land?
8. Name the actors who played Klaatu, Bobby Benson, and Professor Barnhardtt.
9. What is the final "message" Klaatu delivers to the congregation of Earth scientists?
10. The robot will destroy the world unless Helen Benson speaks what words to him?

52. FIRST AND FOREMOST

1. What was the first Ray Harryhausen Dynamation film?
2. Name the first 3-D science fiction movie.
3. When is the first time a death ray appears on film?
4. What is considered to be the first *true* science fiction film?
5. What was the first German sci-fi film?
6. What was the first movie made in 3-D by an English film company?
7. This film, which dealt with miniaturized humans, was considered a notable advance in color trick photography. Name it.
8. The first execution of front projection on a *wide* scale added to the notability of what film?
9. This film represents the first use, by a major studio, of rubber models in animation.
10. What was the first film to employ color animation rear-screen projection?

53. FOUR STARS

Can you identify the film in which these performers acted?

1. Michael Rennie, Patricia Neal, Hugh Marlowe, Sam Jaffe
2. Bradford Dillman, Joanna Miles, Richard Gilliland, Alan Fudge
3. Charlton Heston, Anthony Zerbe, Rosalind Cash, Paul Losio
4. Rock Hudson, Diane Ladd, Barbara Carrera, Roddy McDowall
5. Peter Fonda, Blythe Danner, Arthur Hill, Yul Brynner
6. Michael York, Peter Ustinov, Richard Jordan, Farrah Fawcett-Majors
7. Doug McClure, Peter Cushing, Caroline Munro, Cy Grant
8. Elliot Gould, Trevor Howard, Joseph Bova, Ed Grover
9. George Segal, Joan Hackett, Richard A. Dysart, Jill Clayburgh
10. Donatas Banionis, Nataalya Bondarchuk, Yuri Jarvet, Anatoli Solonitsin

54. "THE WAR OF THE WORLDS"—PART ONE

1. Who is credited with the special effects?
2. By whom was the film directed?
3. *The War of the Worlds* project was first offered to what famous director?
4. Who was the art director?
5. The prologue narration was done by whom?
6. Who wrote the screenplay?
7. This famous English director tried to persuade H. G. Wells to assign him the rights to the novel. Name him.
8. Who designed the costumes?
9. Name the producer.
10. When was the film released and by what company?

55. "THE WAR OF THE WORLDS"—PART TWO

1. The surfaces of what eight planets are depicted at the opening of the film?
2. To what scientific organization does Professor McPherson belong?
3. Why did the Martians decide to invade Earth?
4. What Los Angeles landmark is destroyed by the Martians?
5. What effect does the A-bomb have on the Martians?
6. Who played General Mann?
7. What protects the Martian war machines from cannon fire?
8. Where are Dr. Forrester and Sylvia Van Buren when a Martian is seen?
9. What is the name of the small town where the Martians begin their attack?
10. How are the Martians defeated?

56. THE BOMB

Identify the films described below.

1. A deranged scientist holds London at bay with a bomb of his own manufacture.
2. Only seven people survived this atomic holocaust.
3. This super-bomb was detonated by radio-control from a distance of three thousand miles.
4. There are only three people left after this nuclear explosion.
5. In this serial, Meteorium-245 is the element capable of neutralizing nuclear weapons.
6. An American submarine makes a voyage to Australia to join the survivors of an atomic war.
7. The survivors of atomic warfare come together in a house on a cliff.
8. Simultaneous nuclear tests shift the Earth's orbit.
9. In an atomically destroyed New York, mutations prey on the Normals.
10. A young man crosses a forbidden river in a post-nuclear-war environment.

PHOTO QUIZ

1. Name the two sequels to this film.

2. The result of what disaster, featured in *The Omega Man*, leads Charlton Heston to believe that he is the only survivor of the human race?

3. In *The War of the Worlds*, who destroyed these three emissaries?

4. What actor first portrayed the "Man of Steel" in films?

5. Jean Hagen, Ray Milland, and Frankie Avalon co-starred in this 1962 film about a nuclear holocaust. Name it.

6. What was the name of Captain Nemo's pet seal?

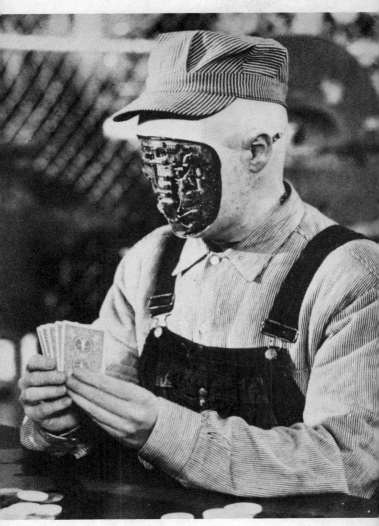

7. This film was the sequel to *Westworld*. Name it.

8. This is a member of what class of society depicted in *Zardoz?*

9. On what planet did Flash Gordon encounter these strange creatures?

10. Best known as TV's Topper, Leo G. Carroll portrayed an ill-fated scientist in what thriller?

11. How did THX-1138 and LUH-3417 fall in love?
12. In what year is this classic sci-fi film set?

13. Identify the actors and the film.

14. What did the crew members of this spaceship discover after landing on a strange planet?

15. Barry Sullivan starred in this American International Pictures production released in 1964. Name it.

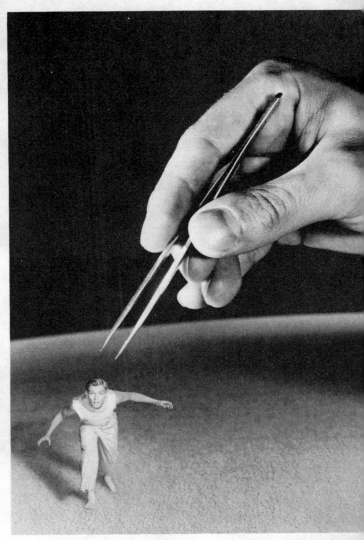

16. On what novel is this sci-fi classic based? Who wrote it?

17. Who played the monster in *Destination Inner Space*?

18. What was Frankenstein's first name?

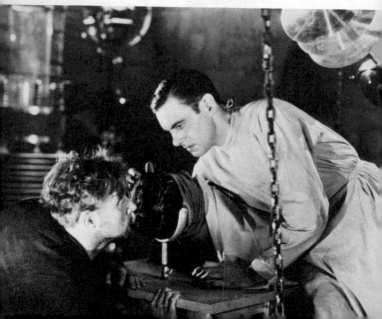

19. Edward G. Robinson's last screen role was in what film?

20. What does the boy fear has happened to his mother?

21. Who created the special effects for this classic?

2001: a space odyssey

MGM PRESENTS A STANLEY KUBRICK PRODUCTION

CINERAMA Super Panavision and Metrocolor

22. How many astronauts were destroyed by HAL 9000 during their voyage to Jupiter?

23. Who produced and directed *"X"—the Man with X-Ray Eyes?*

24. The parents of this little girl were destroyed by what creatures?

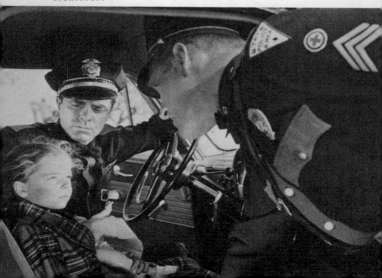

57. SILENCE IS GOLDEN

Match the silent sci-fi film with its producer and release date.

1. *A Trip to the Moon*
2. *A Message From Mars*
3. *The Electric Hotel*
4. *The Third Eye*
5. *The Aerial Submarine*
6. *The Mystery Ship*
7. *The Miracle of Tomorrow*
8. *Through Solid Walls*
9. *The Girl In the Moon*
10. *A Trip to Mars*

a. J. Stuart Blackton, 1908
b. Walter Booth, 1910
c. Universal, 1917
d. Harry Pied, 1923
e. Hayford Hobbs, 1928
f. Jay Belasco, 1916
g. Melies, 1902
h. Edison, 1910
i. UFA, 1929
j. Hollywood, 1910

58. "THX-1138"

1. Who composed the film's score?
2. Why did THX-1138 get into trouble with the authorities?
3. Name the screenwriters.
4. With whom does THX-1138 have an illicit relationship?
5. Who played the title role?
6. Where are religious services held?
7. How are people in this future society identified?
8. Who played the two Chrome Robots?
9. Why does the pursuit of THX-1138 come to a halt?
10. Who was the executive producer, and when was the film released?

59. THE END

Decipher these apocalyptic clues and identify the films.

1. The destruction of the world by a continuous downpour.
2. A scientist penetrates the Earth's crust, ultimately causing the destruction of the planet.
3. The end comes when a comet collides with the world.
4. A missile explodes in space and showers debris upon the Earth.
5. An English village becomes a new satellite when a dead star approaches the Earth.
6. A series of plaques destroys most of mankind.
7. A meteoric bombardment ignites the radiation belt surrounding the Earth.
8. Pollution and a plant virus bring about the end of humanity.
9. A thermonuclear attack has melted the Arctic and is creating a worldwide flood.
10. A new element destroys the Earth from within.

60. THE FIRST TIME AROUND

Each of the following films has been remade at least once. Match the maiden voyage version with its release date.

1. *The Lost World*
2. *20,000 Leagues Under the Sea*
3. *Frankenstein*
4. *Dr. Jekyll and Mr. Hyde*
5. *The Invisible Man*
6. *Island of Dr. Moreau*
7. *Mysterious Island*
8. *From Earth to the Moon*
9. *Alraune* (later known as *Unnatural*)
10. *The First Men in the Moon*

a. 1916 (Verne)
b. 1933 (H. G. Wells)
c. 1908
d. 1933 (Universal)
e. 1929
f. 1925
g. 1902
h. 1910
i. 1919
j. 1927

61. "THE ANDROMEDA STRAIN"

1. Name the author of the source novel.
2. What is the name of the underground installation?
3. What causes victims of the microorganism to die?
4. There are five doctors portrayed in the film. Name them.
5. What is the name of the small town wiped out by the microorganism?
6. Who did the special photographic effects?
7. What will happen if contamination spreads beyond the installation?
8. What is the lowest level of the installation?
9. When and by what company was the film released?
10. How is the alien organism brought to Earth?

62. THE WET ONES

Name the underwater films depicted here.

1. A special submarine is designed to put out a fire in the Van Allen belt.
2. Searching for a lost underwater lab, scientists find a grotto of giant sea creatures.
3. A super-submarine does battle with the invaders from Mu.
4. An asteroid threatens an undersea metropolis of the future.
5. An American girl is kidnapped by "fishmen."
6. Scientists work in an underwater citadel deep beneath the Pacific Ocean.
7. An A-bomb explosion in the Arctic frees a frozen dinosaur.
8. A submerged metropolis is nearly destroyed by an undersea chasm.
9. Scientists in a diving bell find a strange new type of cave.
10. A radiated, mutant manta-ray menaces an undersea city.

63. MONSTER MEN

Match the actor who played a monster with the film in which he appeared.

1. Charles Gemora
2. Glenn Strange
3. Paul Blaisdell

4. Gary Conway
5. Ron Burke

6. Ray "Crash" Corrigan
7. Lock Martin
8. Ricou Browning

9. Jack Le White

10. Paul Blaisdell

a. *It Conquered the World*
b. *Destination Inner Space*
c. *It! The Terror from Beyond Space*
d. *The Day the Earth Stood Still*
e. *The Creature from the Black Lagoon*
f. *The War of the Worlds*
g. *The Day the World Ended*
h. *I Was a Teenage Frankenstein*
i. *Abbott and Costello Meet Frankenstein*
j. *Danny the Dragon*

64. "DESTINATION MOON"

1. The film is based on a book by what famous sci-fi writer?
2. Why was one of the original crewmen unable to make a launch?
3. Who played Dr. Charles Cargraves and General Thayer?
4. Name the producer.
5. What ship takes the astronauts to the moon?
6. Who directed this film?
7. What is their main objective upon landing on the moon?
8. When was the film released?
9. How many astronauts are aboard, and what are their names?
10. As the time for launching approaches, what happens to the project?

65. BIG, BIGGER, BIGGEST

Name the films featuring oversized invaders which are described here.

1. An alien beast starts out as an egg, then grows to monstrous proportions.
2. A monstrous creature is shot from the sky and sinks into the sea.
3. Space monsters hide in a cloud which they have manufactured.
4. Forrest Tucker combats alien invaders.
5. An alien takes over the bodies of people and farm animals.
6. A gelatinous mass from space seeks to devour humanity.
7. An extraterrestrial force has buried itself under the North Pole.
8. An alien from Venus invades Earth.
9. Plants take on huge proportions after a meteor storm.
10. The intentionally funny sequel to the film which featured young Steve McQueen.

66. PLANET MATCH

Match the planet with the film in which it appears.

1. Tralfamador
2. Nova
3. Davanna
4. Rehton
5. Plutonium
6. Mysteroid
7. Mars
8. Lytheon
9. Prometheus 5
10. Astron Delta

a. *King Dinosaur*
b. *The Road to Hong Kong*
c. *The Mysterious*
d. *Rocketship XM*
e. *Barbarella*
f. *Between Time and Timbuktu*
g. *Killers From Space*
h. *Slaughterhouse-Five*
i. *The Phantom Planet*
j. *Not of this Earth*

67. "WHEN WORLDS COLLIDE"

1. In what magazine was the story first serialized?
2. What are the names of the two runaway planets?
3. The film was first offered to what famous director?
4. Who discovers that the planets are heading on a collision course with Earth?
5. How many days are allowed for outfitting and launching the *Ark*?
6. Which planet will destroy the Earth completely?
7. Name the film's producer.
8. Why is Sydney Stanton allowed on the *Ark*?
9. When will the first planet create havoc on Earth?
10. How many people will be taken aboard the *Ark*?

68. TV OR NOT TV

Name the TV series described here.

1. A group of adventurers stumble onto an island which exists in a space-time continuum.
2. First syndicated in the early fifties, this series featured George Reeves in the title role.
3. The hero of this short-lived series could maintain his "condition" for a brief length of time.
4. This man's life is saved and, in the process, he becomes a cyborg.
5. This doctor must do battle with aliens known as the Silurians.
6. The protagonist of this program, a newspaperman, discovers vampires and other strange creatures.
7. This secret organization was formed to combat cosmic invaders and safeguard United States atomic secrets.
8. This man was the "Guardian of the Safety of the World" in the future-world of 2254.
9. This show followed the exploits of the "Sky Marshall of the Universe."
10. An alien from this series had one flaw—a crooked finger on the right hand.

69. FUTURE STARS

Each of these artists toiled in the sci-fi field before achieving renown. Match the man with his early credit.

1. Clint Eastwood
2. Lloyd Bridges
3. James Arness
4. Leonard Nimoy
5. Steve McQueen
6. Elmer Bernstein
7. Humphrey Bogart

8. Tom Tryon
9. Peter Graves
10. Earl Holliman

a. *Zombies of the Stratosphere*
b. *Tarantula*
c. *Return of Dr. X*
d. *Killers from Space*
e. *The Forbidden Planet*
f. *Rocketship XM*
g. *I Married a Monster from Outer Space*
h. *The Blob*
i. *The Thing*
j. *Robot Monster*

70. "20,000 LEAGUES UNDER THE SEA"

1. Who portrayed Ned Land and Conseil?
2. How is the *Nautilus* powered?
3. When was the film released?
4. Who played Captain Nemo?
5. Name the director.
6. What is the *Nautilus*'s home port?
7. Who created the special effects?
8. The *Nautilus* is attacked by what undersea denizen?
9. Who composed the music?
10. What musical instrument does Nemo play during the quieter moments of the patrol?

71. RADIO, RADIO

Can you name the classic radio series described here?

1. This was one of the first radio programs to be recorded on tape. It featured such stars as Art Carney and Jack Lemmon.
2. This series was first heard on the Mutual Network in 1945, and featured Orson Welles in an episode entitled "The Battle Never Ends."
3. Based on a well-known comic strip, this show featured Gale Gordon as the redoubtable hero.
4. This crime-fighting hero once saved a metropolis from destruction by a deadly ray gun.
5. This show featured the adventures of Captain Craig McKensie and his super submarine.
6. Listeners could become "Solar Scouts" and receive "planetary maps" by responding to the premium offers of this popular serial.
7. On Sunday evening, October 30, 1938, this dramatization of a science fiction story created panic among many of the listeners.
8. The hero of this serial was a brilliant scientist whose advanced experiments enabled him to catch criminals.
9. This program featured a "strange visitor from another planet" who made it his career to fight crime.
10. This show was first broadcast in 1950 as a response to the nation's growing interest in science fiction.

72. MAKING A LIVING

Describe the professions these actors practiced in these films.

1. Richard Carlson in *It Came From Outer Space*
2. Roger St. Luc in *They Came From Within*
3. Robert Vaughn in *The Mind of Mr. Soames*
4. Donald Pleasance in *The Mutation*
5. Eric Braeden in *Colossus: The Forbin Project*
6. Drew Pearson in *The Day the Earth Stood Still*
7. George Pal in *The War of the Worlds*
8. Laura Hippe in *Logan's Run*
9. Peter Cushing in *At the Earth's Core*
10. Ralph Meeker in *Food of the Gods*

73. "ZARDOZ"

1. In what year does the film take place?
2. What is Zardoz?
3. Who wrote, produced and directed this film?
4. What does May's examination of Zed reveal?
5. Who portrayed Zed and Consuella?
6. What replaces sleep in the lush region?
7. What two regions are the future society divided into?
8. How does Zed destroy the Zardoz?
9. What are the people called who inhabit the lush region?
10. Who was director of photography?

74. BUCK ROGERS

1. This serial was based on what 1928 novel?
2. At the beginning, Buck Rogers wakes up and finds himself how far into the future?
3. What enables Buck to live so long?
4. Who portrayed the first Buck Rogers?
5. Who is the master of the evil forces?
6. Name three weapons in the arsenal of the leader of the good forces.
7. Who wrote the novel upon which the serial is based?
8. How does Buck become a robot?
9. With whom does he join forces in the battle against evil?
10. Who are the henchmen of the evil forces' master, and where do they come from?

75. MOVIE MAGICIANS

Match the special effects genius with his film project.

1.	John D. Fulton	a.	*Project Moonbase*
2.	Jacques Fresco	b.	*Monster from Green Hall*
3.	Fred Sersen	c.	*Forbidden Planet*
4.	Glen Robinson	d.	*The Man Who Fell to Earth*
5.	Roy Arbogast	e.	*The Space Children*
6.	Jack Rabin	f.	*Journey to the Seventh Planet*
7.	Jim Danforth	g.	*Destination Moon*
8.	Gene Warren	h.	*Unknown World*
9.	A. Arnold Gillespie	i.	*The Day the Earth Stood Still*
10.	P. S. Ellenshaw	j.	*Embryo*

76. "FANTASTIC PLANET"

1. The film is a result of a co-production between what two countries?
2. The story is set on what planet?
3. Who are the Oms?
4. Name the director.
5. What was the name of the adopted baby Om?
6. The film is based on what novel?
7. How tall are the Draags?
8. How do the Oms destroy the Draags?
9. Who was the chief animator?
10. What color are the Draags' eyes?

77. ROBOT

Can you identify the films from these cryptic clues?

1. A giant robot from space destroys several Japanese cities.
2. Two robots turn on their masters and are eliminated.
3. A robot is built to withstand the stress of space travel.
4. A young lad is kidnapped by a robot.
5. A man wakes up after a robot invasion to find his town deserted.
6. A woman switches roles with a robot.
7. A gorilla wearing a space helmet arrives on Earth.
8. A man discovers he's been turned into a robot.
9. A mechanical monster battles an ape atop Tokyo Towers.
10. A man's brain is transplanted to a twelve-foot robot.

78. CINEMA SCRIBES

Match the screenwriter with his film.

1. Robett J. Jaffe
2. Ray Bradbury
3. David Z. Goodman
4. Ted Sherdeman
5. Earl Felton
6. John William and
   Joyce Corrington
7. Stephen Geller
8. James Bridges
9. Parel Juracek and
   J. Polak

10. Stirling Silliphant,
    W. Rilla, and
    George Barclay

a. *The Omega Man*
b. *Demon Seed*
c. *Slaughterhouse-Five*
d. *Colossus: The Forbin Project*
e. *Them!*

f. *20,000 Leagues Under the Sea*
g. *The Illustrated Man*
h. *Village of the Damned*

i. *Voyage to the End of the
   Universe*

j. *Logan's Run*

79. "SILENT RUNNING"

1. Why has the Earth been defoliated?
2. What are the names of the two drones who wind up in the dome with Lowell?
3. What company was responsible for the space vehicles?
4. This film was a directorial debut for what special effects man?
5. What credo does Lowell have taped to his bunk?
6. What is the name of the ship that carries the four central characters?
7. Once Lowell is free of the Berkshire fleet, what planet causes him trouble?
8. Who performed the songs for the film?
9. Which drone is obliterated with Lowell at the film's conclusion?
10. What environment is represented in Lowell's dome?

80. ON THE AIR

Can you identify these television series?

1. Enroute from New York to London, a suborbital ship encounters an electrical storm which places the seven occupants in an unknown world.
2. While exploring the Colorado River, a forest ranger and his children become caught in a time vortex.
3. This family embarks on the *Jupiter II* in search of a new planet to colonize, and, in the process, loses its way.
4. The androids Fi and Fum from the planet ZR-3 accidentally find themselves on Earth.
5. Witnessing the crash of a U.F.O., a newspaper reporter discovers and befriends its passenger.
6. This science fiction anthology series was first syndicated in 1951, and featured programs derived from pulp magazine short stories.
7. This short-lived show was based on a film which spawned four sequels.
8. This group of adventurers occupied the Omega Base for its exploration of the unknown regions of space.
9. Host-narrator Truman Bradley introduced each story with a scientific explanation for the premise.
10. Three hundred men and women are adrift on a satellite in this recent series, acclaimed for its special effects.

81. "DARK STAR"

1. Which bomb fails to eject from the ship?
2. Name the actors who portrayed Pinback, Doolittle, and Boiler.
3. The film was started as a production at what United States university?
4. What is the mission of the crew of the *Dark Star*?
5. Who was killed at the beginning of the mission and is kept in suspended animation?
6. How is the bomb "argued" out of exploding?
7. What was Ron Cobb's contribution to this film?
8. Who was the producer, director, and co-writer?
9. What does Pinback use to "coax" the alien mascot back into its room?
10. Who was the special effects designer?

82. MOVIES EOR TV
—PART ONE

Identify the television movies described here.

1. Race car driver Ben Richards discovers that his blood has unusual qualities.
2. A distraught couple learns that they have been misled by secret agents with advanced electronic gear.
3. The outcome of World War Three is decided by representatives who battle to the death.
4. Aliens from two warring planets take human form to fight it out on Earth.
5. A whole town is in bondage to aliens.
6. Human beings are used for guinea pigs in a mad experiment.
7. A brilliant genetic scientist discovers a way to alter hereditary factors to increase intelligence.
8. In a future world, strict controls are placed on reproduction.
9. An evil genius seeks to rule the world.
10. A concerned wife hires a special researcher who discovers her husband was murdered by a telepath.

83. MOVIES FOR TV
—PART TWO

Name the movies made for TV that are described below.

1. Ernest Borgnine has an android for a partner.
2. Richard Boone plays a ruthless millionaire who goes on the ultimate safari.
3. The adventures of the captain of a United Galaxy Sanitation Patrol ship.
4. A family's interstellar voyage goes off course.
5. This film involves a mysterious being from an advanced society.
6. Insects from south of the border invade the United States.
7. On a camping trip, a family discovers that humanity has been wiped out by a solar fire.
8. Three astronauts find themselves on Earth after spending 180 years in space.
9. Adventurers find themselves in the midst of the infamous Chicago fire.
10. This film recounts the story of a couple who is examined by beings from another planet.

84. MUSIC MEN

Match the composer with the film for which he provided original music.

1. Louis and Bébé
   Barron
2. Gene Garf
3. Dmitri Tiomkin
4. Bernard Herrmann
5. Charles Fox
6. Leith Stevens
7. John Morris
8. Angelo Lavagnino
9. Paul Sawtell
10. Russell Garcia

a. *Forbidden Planet*
b. *The Thing*
c. *The Fly*
d. *Bug*
e. *King Dinosaur*
f. *The Day the Earth Stood Still*
g. *Young Frankenstein*
h. *Gorgo*
i. *When Worlds Collide*
j. *The Time Machine*

85. "A BOY AND HIS DOG"

1. In what year is the film set?
2. Name the band of human scavengers who roam the surface.
3. What was the dog's name?
4. Downunder is modeled after what city?
5. Who provided the voice of the dog?
6. Who portrayed Vic?
7. Who was the art director?
8. What award did the novella this film was based upon win?
9. Who portrayed Lew?
10. Name the film's director.

86. SERIAL TIME

Can you identify these serials from the clues provided?

1. Tristam Coffin was the futuristic hero in this late-forties Republic serial.
2. The first serial to combine super-science with the fable of sunken Atlantis.
3. Gene Autry was an unwilling captive in this Mascot serial.
4. The Iron Terror was a mechanical monster in a serial featuring a famous magician.
5. The "X-Ray Eye" and the "X-Ray Belt" were two typical episodes.
6. A black-coated Lightning fires electrical thunderbolts at the hero.
7. Dr. Topor had to reckon with two heroes of this serial when he created his destructive Fusion Force.
8. Baroda's Electro-Annihilator was featured.
9. The Spider Lady is destroyed with her own weapon.
10. The villain of this series could transmute rocks into gold.

87. AUTHOR! AUTHOR!

Match the movie with the author whose work is its source.

1. *The Time Machine*
2. *Fahrenheit 451*
3. *A Boy and His Dog*
4. *20,000 Leagues Under the Sea*
5. *Solaris*
6. *1984*
7. *The Man Who Fell to Earth*
8. *Robinson Crusoe on Mars*
9. *Charly*
10. *Planet of the Apes*

a. Daniel Keyes
b. Pierre Boulle
c. Harlan Ellison
d. Stanislas Lem
e. Jules Verne
f. Ray Bradbury
g. Walter Tevis
h. H. G. Wells
i. George Orwell
j. Daniel Defoe

88. "WIZARDS"

1. What was the name of the evil sorcerer?
2. List Ralph Bakshi's three previous films.
3. Who accompanies the good brother on his quest?
4. What is the name of the peaceful side of the planet?
5. Who was the director of photography?
6. What is the source of the evil sorcerer's power?
7. Who composed the music?
8. What does the evil sorcerer find in the ruins of an ancient city?
9. What is the name of the evil sorcerer's factory?
10. What is the good brother's name?

89. FRANKLY FRANKENSTEIN

Arrange these *Frankenstein* movies in order of their release.

a. *Frankenstein Meets the Wolf Man*
b. *House of Frankenstein*
c. *Curse of Frankenstein*
d. *Revenge of Frankenstein*
e. *Evil of Frankenstein*
f. *Frankenstein's Daughter*
g. *Frankenstein Created Woman*
h. *Horror of Frankenstein*
i. *Blood of Frankenstein*
j. *Young Frankenstein*

90. LIGHTS! CAMERA! ACTION!

Match the director with his sci-fi film.

1. Richard Carlson
2. Jean-Luc Godard
3. Roger Corman
4. George Roy Hill
5. François Truffaut
6. Robert Wise
7. Freddie Francis
8. Arthur C. Pierce
9. Inoshiro Honda
10. Peter Watkins

a. *Alphaville*
b. *The Andromeda Strain*
c. *Trog*
d. *Not of This Earth*
e. *Yog—Monster from Space*
f. *Riders to the Stars*
g. *Slaughterhouse-Five*
h. *Fahrenheit 451*
i. *The War Game*
j. *Women of the Prehistoric Planet*

91. "WESTWORLD"

1. What is the name of the adult recreation complex?
2. Who is bitten by the robot snake?
3. Who wrote and directed this film?
4. Who saves the "woman" from torture in the dungeon?
5. When and by what company was the film released?
6. Who played the gunslinger robot?
7. When do Peter and John start accepting Westworld as real?
8. What three periods are created in the amusement park?
9. Who ordered the vodka martini in the saloon?
10. Who portrayed Peter Martin and John Blane?

92. MEN INTO MONSTERS

Can you name these monstrous films?

1. A scientist hopes to grow new limbs on people with a serum derived from an amphibious reptile.
2. A man is caught in an atomic explosion while trying to rescue a friend.
3. An oversized man is blasted by a bazooka and returns to wreak havoc.
4. A jealous giant destroys herself and her husband.
5. A man and a guinea pig become "inter-mixed."
6. A scientist becomes a scale-caked monster when exposed to sunlight.
7. An alien life-form transforms an astronaut into a giant fungus.
8. A convict is brought back to life for revenge.
9. A scientist revives the dead for evil purposes.
10. A man's "evil-self" becomes personified, and breaks from his body.

93. "ROLLERBALL"

1. In what time period is the film set?
2. Who maintains the game for the people?
3. Who produced and directed this film?
4. Which organization sponsors Jonathan E's team?
5. Describe the team.
6. Who is Jonathan E's trainer?
7. Why is Jonathan E in trouble with the rulers who maintain the game?
8. Who played Jonathan E?
9. What is the name of the computer?
10. What is the title of the short story on which the film is based?

94. MISS CASTING

Match the actress with the film in which she appeared.

1. Claire Bloom
2. Julie Christie
3. Suzanne Pleshette
4. Connie Stevens
5. Zsa Zsa Gabor
6. Veronica Lake
7. Anne Francis
8. Jane Fonda
9. Raquel Welch
10. Ursula Andress

a. *The Tenth Victim*
b. *Barbarella*
c. *Queen of Outer Space*
d. *The Satan Bug*
e. *Flesh Feast*
f. *The Power*
g. *Fantastic Voyage*
h. *Way . . . Way Out*
i. *The Illustrated Man*
j. *Demon Seed*

95. INVADERS—PART ONE

Name the films described here.

1. A flying saucer is discovered beneath the Arctic surface.
2. Two American scientists are kidnapped and taken to a world at war.
3. A warning is presented to Earth on the misuse of atomic energy.
4. An invader wore a trench coat and dark glasses.
5. This invader terrorized a ski lodge.
6. Aliens visit Earth in search of zombies.
7. A group of invaders is betrayed when one of their number falls in love with an Earth girl.
8. An invader takes over John Agar's body.
9. An invisible alien invades Earth.
10. A giant brain takes over children whose parents are important research scientists.

96. INVADERS—PART TWO

From these brief descriptions, identify the films.

1. Aliens import giant insects and lizards for the invasion of Earth.
2. Inhabitants of a small Scottish town are to be hypnotized for a future invasion.
3. A TV set "invades" Earth and spawns a horde of miniature TV receivers.
4. An alien rides to Earth aboard a satellite.
5. Beings from space give capsules to a select group of Earthlings.
6. Crystals from space turn people into stone.
7. Aliens enslave the will of Earthlings.
8. A mutant female from the future visits the 20th century.
9. Aliens seek to sabotage a satellite project.
10. Bug-eyed beings are controlled by a small, tentacled creature in a glass dome.

97. "THE MAN WHO FELL TO EARTH"

1. Who is the first Earthman that Newton encounters?
2. What character does David Bowie play?
3. Identify at least three songs which are included in the soundtrack.
4. Who wrote the screenplay?
5. What is the name of Newton's home planet?
6. Who was the musical director?
7. Who directed the film?
8. What happens to Newton's eyes?
9. Who is Newton's attorney?
10. While Bryce and Mary Lou are discussing Newton's fate, what film is he watching?

98. DON'T BUG ME

Match the insect-ridden film with its description.

1. *The Wasp Woman*

2. *Phase IV*

3. *The Deadly Mantis*

4. *Beginning of the End*

5. *Tarantula*

6. *The Black Scorpion*

7. *Earth Versus The Spider*

8. *Monster That Challenged the World*

9. *Bug*

10. *The Fly*

a. A gigantic spider terrorizes a town (1955)

b. Scientists do battle with an intelligent ant civilization

c. Giant caterpillars invade Southern California through irrigation canals

d. Humanity vs. a triple threat: giant spider, scorpion and a clawed worm

e. A newly thawed, giant praying mantis threatens a U. S. city

f. She wanted to stay young with a flying insect's enzyme

g. Hybrid cockroaches set people ablaze

h. A scientist switches an arm and leg with a winged insect

i. Giant locusts and vegetables on the rampage

j. Another gigantic spider terrorizes another town (1958)

99. "THINGS TO COME"

1. What is the name of the ravaged city?
2. Who directed the film?
3. Who built the models for the film?
4. What two major events did the film predict?
5. Who is John Cable's son?
6. Who wrote the screenplay?
7. How is the end of the war brought about?
8. John Cable was the leader of what organization?
9. Who got launched into space by the space gun?
10. When and in what country was the film released?

100. THE SCI-FI CONNOISSEUR'S QUIZ

1. Name the invaders who attack Exeter's plane in *This Island Earth*.
2. Where did *The Beast With a Million Eyes* first arrive on Earth?
3. What are the names of the two robots in *Gog*?
4. Exeter was an emissary from what planet?
5. Who played the monster in *Zaat*?
6. What is *Danny the Dragon* looking for?
7. What is the name of the monkey companion of Paul Mantee in *Robinson Crusoe On Mars*?
8. Name the space station infected by a fungus in *Mutiny in Outer Space*.
9. Florence Marly plays what character in *Queen of Blood*?
10. What is the name of the robot in *Devil Girl From Mars*?
11. Who played the "Mutant" in *This Island Earth*?

ANSWERS

QUIZ 1

1. i
2. h
3. f
4. a
5. g
6. d
7. j
8. c
9. e
10. b

QUIZ 2

1. g
2. e
3. f
4. a
5. d
6. i
7. j
8. h
9. c
10. b

QUIZ 3

1. Beru Lars to her husband Owen after he and Luke have argued about Luke's going to the Academy
2. Bartender refusing to serve C-3PO and R2-D2 in the cantina
3. Princess Leia to Chewbacca while they are making their escape from the *Death Star*
4. A drunken space pirate to Luke in the cantina
5. C-3PO to himself as they prepare to go into hyper-space after escaping Tatooine
6. Han Solo to the bartender after he has destroyed Greedo
7. C-3PO to R2-D2 after their landing on Tatooine
8. Princess Leia to Han Solo after seeing the *Millennium Falcon*
9. Ben Kenobi to Han Solo after they have been captured by the *Death Star*
10. C-3PO to R2-D2 while under attack by the Imperial cruiser that captures the Princess

QUIZ 4

1. Twenty years old
2. A suggestion from C-3PO
3. Luke wants to leave the farm for the Academy
4. While cleaning him
5. The Princess, although Kenobi telepathically persuades him also
6. While learning to use the lightsaber aboard the *Millennium Falcon*
7. Two
8. By suggesting that his reward may be "more wealth than you can imagine"
9. After his aunt and uncle have been murdered by the stormtroopers
10. By the appearance of Ben (Obi-Wan) Kenobi

QUIZ 5

1. He died about the same time as Luke's father
2. By imitating the call of a Krayt dragon
3. A cave
4. That he deliver R2-D2 safely to her father
5. General Obi-Wan Kenobi
6. He served with the Old Republic during the Clone Wars
7. In a lightsaber duel with Darth Vader
8. Before Luke's birth
9. They were close friends
10. "If you strike me down, I will only become more powerful than you can imagine"

QUIZ 6

1. Princess and Royal Senator of the Old Republic
2. Viceroy and First Chairman of the Alderaan System
3. The world family of Alderaan and the Alliance to Restore the Republic
4. Bail Organa
5. Alderaan
6. Dantooine
7. She was on "a diplomatic mission"
8. Cell 2187
9. By locating and using the hatch-door switch
10. At the display screen in the rebel headquarters

QUIZ 7

1. Corellian
2. The *Millennium Falcon*
3. Docking bay 94
4. "Parsecs"
5. 17,000
6. Jabba the Hut
7. Greedo
8. Smuggling
9. Two
10. By causing a collision between the Tie-fighters which are pursuing Luke

QUIZ 8

1. He speaks Bocce and can program vaporators
2. Human-cyborg relations
3. He is afraid he will be deactivated
4. After losing his arm in an attack of the Sandpeople
5. At the rebel command post operations room
6. His left arm
7. He mistakes their salvage vessel for a rescue mission unit
8. In Ben Kenobi's cave home
9. Placing a dead Jawa on a funeral pyre
10. By claiming that he is taking R2-D2 to the maintenance shop

QUIZ 9

1. One
2. An Astromech android
3. He suggests that if it is removed, Luke will be able to see the entire message for Ben Kenobi
4. Three
5. To get the Princess's message to Ben Kenobi
6. One meter (or 39.37 inches)
7. Computer repair and information retrieval
8. With Luke aboard the X-wing fighter
9. A damaged stabilizer
10. Six

QUIZ 10

1. A Wookie
2. Blue
3. A bandolier
4. First Mate
5. "Chewie"
6. Cellblock TS-138
7. He is losing a game to R2-D2 aboard the spacefreighter
8. He growls softly at her
9. In the cantina at Mos Eisley
10. One hundred years old

QUIZ 11

1. Dark Lord of the Sith
2. A Jedi Knight
3. Ben (Obi-Wan) Kenobi
4. Black
5. A black cape
6. He lifts him off his feet and chokes him to death
7. With "the Force"
8. The rebel fighters are so small that they are evading the fixed guns
9. The *Millennium Falcon*'s markings identify it as the ship that escaped Tatooine
10. Gold Two

QUIZ 12

1. Governor of the outlying Imperial Territories
2. Gray-green
3. Two
4. The *Death Star*
5. When they capture the *Millennium Falcon*, they decide to use the Princess to help them find the tapes
6. Darth Vader
7. Threatening to blow up her home planet
8. Dantooine is too far from the centers of Imperial populations to serve as the subject of an effective hit
9. A homing beacon has been placed on the craft
10. Because it is his "moment of triumph"

QUIZ 13

1. f
2. h
3. j or b
4. i
5. g
6. e
7. c
8. b or j
9. a
10. d

QUIZ 14

1. Red
2. At Ben Kenobi's cave home
3. Knowledge of "the Force" and how to use it
4. Supralight jump
5. One meter (or 39.37 inches)
6. Blue
7. Prototropic shielding
8. 117891
9. "Point five past Lightspeed"
10. Pink

QUIZ 15

1. Guardians of justice under the Old Republic
2. A commander of the Imperial forces
3. A rebel fighter pilot who loses his life on a run against the *Death Star*
4. An Imperial commander aboard the *Death Star*
5. Commander of the rebel fighter squadrons
6. Luke Skywalker's aunt
7. Leader of the rebel forces
8. Captain Antilles
9. Nomadic desert dwellers of Tatooine, also known as Sandpeople
10. R2-D2

QUIZ 16

1. Information tapes on the structural details of the *Death Star*
2. The small farming community where Luke lives with his aunt and uncle
3. Tatoo I and Tatoo II
4. Yellow
5. "The force can have a strong influence on a weak mind"
6. Massive horned creatures used as mounts
7. Android plating
8. The Jedi Knights
9. THX-1138
10. The bleached-out skeleton of an enormous beast

QUIZ 17

1. After he and R2-D2 argue and split up over the proper direction to take in the Tatooine wastelands
2. During the Clone Wars
3. Before breakfast, the night after R2-D2 escapes
4. After the Princess's message is delivered in Ben Kenobi's home
5. At the awards ceremony after the final battle
6. On the catwalk, just before they swing across on a cable
7. When he is ambushed by the Jawas
8. When the emergency alert is sounded in the Princess's detention block
9. Before Luke leaves the rebel base to do battle with the Imperials
10. At the briefing of the fighter pilots before the final battle.

QUIZ 18

1. Stunned by an explosion, he lies in a corridor
2. The irrigation units on the south ridge
3. In the hold of the Jawas' scavenger vehicle
4. Into the Jundland wastes of Tatooine
5. Mos Eisley
6. The spice mines of Kessel
7. At home eating dinner
8. Bestine
9. In a cantina
10. On a satellite of the planet Yavin

QUIZ 19

1. The sought-after plans of the *Death Star* might be aboard
2. His original choice breaks down before the Jawas leave
3. The Sandpeople are most dangerous at night
4. He mistakes their cries of relief for the sound of agony
5. R2-D2 has been hit by Darth Vader's ship
6. Ben Kenobi advises him to use "the Force"
7. He feels a great loss when Alderaan is destroyed
8. It smells bad
9. Because the garbage hold has been activated to crush its contents
10. They may end up in a Super-Nova

QUIZ 20

1. By faking a distress signal which claims the ship was destroyed by a meteor storm
2. He was betrayed, then murdered by Darth Vader
3. By selling his landspeeder
4. By luring it close enough to be caught by a tractor beam
5. By having R2-D2 plug into the ship and shut down all the garbage units
6. The Bantha tracks are side by side, not single file
7. By dissolving the Imperial Senate
8. By setting off a chain reaction in the ship's reactor core
9. By their cloak design
10. R2-D2 finds out from the ship's computers, then informs Luke

QUIZ 21

1. g
2. i
3. a
4. d
5. h
6. b
7. e
8. c
9. f
10. j

QUIZ 22

1. False (Han Solo is awarded the first medal)
2. False (Darth Vader spins out of control in space and escapes final destruction of the *Death Star*)
3. False (At Mos Eisley he says, "I can't abide those Jawas")
4. False (Luke has no brother)
5. False
6. True
7. False (The rebel base is located on one of the moons of Yavin)
8. False (She never reveals the secret)
9. True
10. False (It destroys Alderaan)

QUIZ 23

1. Thirty-three (born May 14, 1944)
2. Four years
3. U.S.C.
4. Assistant to the director
5. *THX-1138*
6. San Anselmo, California
7. *American Graffiti*
8. Alex Raymond, who created the *Flash Gordon* series
9. Eleven million dollars
10. Nine hundred

QUIZ 24

1. f
2. g
3. i
4. h
5. j
6. b
7. d
8. e
9. a
10. c

QUIZ 25

1. The magnetic field of the *Death Star*
2. Red Leader
3. Red Five
4. "Shooting wamp rats in his T-16 back home"
5. When Biggs is unable to escape a pursuing Tie-fighter
6. Red Four (John D)
7. Red Two (Wedge)
8. Three marks at 210
9. Red Leader
10. Luke, Wedge, and Biggs

QUIZ 26

1. Maria (played by Brigitte Helm)
2. Fritz Lang
3. 2000
4. Forty million marks
5. John Fredersen
6. Theda von Harbou
7. 1927; Germany; UFA
8. Rotwang
9. A mob of incensed workers smash the machines which control the water supply, flooding the lower levels
10. Karl Freund and Gunter Rittau

QUIZ 27

1. Mobula
2. Mothra *(Godzilla vs. The Thing, et al)*
3. Daleks *(Daleks—Invasion Earth 2150 A.D., et al)*
4. Gorgo *(Gorgo)*
5. Gor *(The Brain from Planet Arous)*
6. Ymir *(20 Million Miles to Earth)*
7. Gamera *(Gamera Versus Jiger)*
8. Gargon *(Teenagers from Outer Space)*
9. Proteus *(Demon Seed)*
10. Medra *(Blood Beast from Outer Space)*

QUIZ 28

1. b
2. a
3. h
4. j
5. i
6. c
7. e
8. d
9. f
10. g

QUIZ 29

1. 1956; Allied Artists
2. Don Siegel
3. Jack Finney
4. Santa Mira
5. Kevin McCarthy; Dr. Miles Bennell
6. A gas-meter reader, or, as he called himself in the film, "the gasman"
7. Dana Wynter; Becky Driscoll
8. Carmen Dragon
9. Three: at the greenhouse, in his car, and in his office
10. Milt Rice

QUIZ 30

1. *X—the Man with X-Ray Eyes*
2. *Q Planes*
3. *Batman and Robin,* a serial
4. *The 4-D Man*
5. *The Whispering Shadow,* a serial
6. *Dr. No*
7. *The Crazy Ray*
8. *Murder at Dawn*
9. *Shadow of the Eagle*
10. *Daredevils of the Red Circle,* a serial

QUIZ 31

1. h
2. f
3. j
4. g
5. i
6. a
7. e
8. b
9. d
10. c

QUIZ 32

1. James Whitmore, James Arness, Fess Parker, and Leonard Nimoy, respectively
2. George Worthing Yates
3. 1954; Warner Brothers
4. Gordon Douglas
5. In the storm drains beneath Los Angeles
6. Radioactivity from an A-bomb test
7. In the Mohave Desert
8. Dr. Patricia Medford
9. Flamethrowers
10. The terrified screams of a little girl

QUIZ 33

1. *Life in the Next Century*
2. *Charleston*
3. *Just Imagine*
4. *The Airship*
5. *Fahrenheit 451*
6. *One Hundred Years After*
7. *Project X*
8. *The Illustrated Man*
9. *Midnight Menace*
10. *1984*

QUIZ 34

1. f
2. d
3. i
4. a and h
5. c
6. b and k
7. e
8. g
9. j

QUIZ 35

1. A needle
2. Jack Arnold
3. 1957; Universal
4. Advertising executive
5. Carey almost drowns
6. Richard Matheson
7. He continues to shrink into the infinitesimal cosmos
8. Grant Williams and Randy Stuart
9. In an accident involving exposure to radiation and an insecticide
10. Clifford Stine, Roswell A. Hoffman, and Everett H. Broussard

QUIZ 36

1. False (The novel was written by Richard Matheson)
2. False (It was an American and Soviet Union computer)
3. True
4. True
5. False
6. False (Lon Chaney, Jr., was not in the film)
7. False (The film was produced by Kurt Newman)
8. True
9. True
10. True

QUIZ 37

1. d
2. h
3. j
4. c
5. a
6. e
7. g
8. b
9. f
10. i

QUIZ 38

1. *The Tempest*
2. Fred McLeod Wilcox
3. Altair IV
4. Altaira (played by Anne Francis)
5. United Space Cruiser C-57D
6. The demonic spirit of Morbius
7. The Krel
8. Robby (played by Frankie Carpenter)
9. $1,900,000
10. 1956; M.G.M.

QUIZ 39

1. Alex Raymond
2. "Flash Gordon," "Flash Gordon's Trip to Mars," and "Flash Gordon Conquers the Universe"
3. Frederick Stephani
4. Mongo
5. Jean Rogers
6. Lionmen, Sharkmen, Hawkmen, Octosacs, Orangopoids, and Tigrons
7. Ming the Merciless
8. A Nitron Lamp
9. Azura, Queen of Mars
10. Treemen and Clay People

QUIZ 40

1. d
2. e
3. f
4. g
5. b
6. h
7. i
8. a
9. j
10. c

QUIZ 41

1. A Venus probe returns with an unknown form of radiation which activates the dead
2. Judith O'Dea and Russell Streiner
3. She is immolated in a flaming truck
4. 1968
5. George A. Romero
6. After she escapes from one of the dead and hides in a small farmhouse
7. He is mistaken for the living dead and shot by the police
8. None
9. John A. Russo
10. In the cemetery

QUIZ 42

1. *Planet of the Apes;* Taylor
2. *Planet of the Apes* (1967), *Beneath the Planet of the Apes* (1969), *Escape from the Planet of the Apes* (1970), *Conquest of the Planet of the Apes* (1972), and *Battle for the Planet of the Apes* (1973)
3. *Planet of the Apes;* Best Original Score and Costume Design
4. Twentieth Century-Fox
5. Franklin J. Schaffner
6. Arthur P. Jacobs
7. Rod Serling and Michael Wilson
8. Taylor
9. *The Bridge on the River Kwai*
10. *Planet of the Apes* and *Beneath the Planet of the Apes*

QUIZ 43

1. *Planet of Man*
2. U.S.C.
3. The Statue of Liberty
4. Jerry Goldsmith
5. Taylor
6. Paul Dehn
7. *Beneath the Planet of the Apes*
8. Maurice Evans
9. Zira, Cornelius, and Milo
10. All but *Beneath the Planet of the Apes*

QUIZ 44

1. Caesar
2. *Planet of the Apes, Beneath the Planet of the Apes,* and *Escape from the Planet of the Apes*
3. Ricardo Montalban
4. Ted Post, Don Taylor, and—the last two—J. Lee Thompson
5. Aldo
6. Kelp
7. He was afraid he'd give Caesar away to the police
8. John Huston
9. From falling off a branch cut from underneath him by Aldo
10. In a devastated city populated by mutants

QUIZ 45

1. a; *Things to Come*
2. i; *Fahrenheit 451*
3. d; *1984*
4. j; *Flesh Gordon*
5. e; *The Mysterious Island*
6. b; *Flash Gordon*
7. g; *Flight to Mars*
8. h; *Those Fantastic Flying Fools*
9. f; *Solaris*
10. c; *Horror of the Blood Monsters*

QUIZ 46

1. "The Sentinel"; Arthur C. Clarke
2. The signal from the monolith on the moon is traced to the vicinity of Jupiter
3. Wally Veevers, Douglas Trumbull, and Con Pederson
4. Poole (played by Gary Lockwood)
5. Pan Am
6. Three
7. Douglas Rain
8. Smyslov
9. A telemetry antenna
10. Richard Strauss, Gyorgy Ligeti, Johann Strauss, and Aram Khachaturian

QUIZ 47

1. Nothing wrong
2. Television set
3. Adjust the picture
4. Transmission
5. Control
6. See
7. Hear
8. Participate in a great adventure
9. Experience the awe and mystery
10. Outer limits

QUIZ 48

1. Alcohol
2. Junior
3. Gene Fowler
4. On his way home from his bachelor party
5. The sending clerk tears up the message
6. Tom Tryon and Gloria Talbott
7. A cat
8. Grady
9. After leaving their nighttime reception, Bill drives for a long period without lights
10. 1958; Paramount

QUIZ 49

1. *Things to Come*
2. *The Thing*
3. *Destination Moon*
4. *Invasion of the Bee Girls*
5. *The Black Scorpion*
6. *Crack in the World*
7. *Flesh Feast*
8. *A Blind Bargain*
9. *Children of the Damned*
10. *Return of the Fly*

QUIZ 50

1. *A Trip to the Moon;* George Méliés
2. *A Trip to Mars;* Frederick Jacobsen
3. *The First Men in the Moon;* Hector Abbas
4. *Flash Gordon;* Charles Middleton
5. *Things to Come;* Raymond Massey
6. *Destination Moon;* Warner Anderson
7. *Metropolis;* Rudolf Klein-Rogge
8. *Rocketship XM;* John Emery
9. *The Thing;* Douglas Spencer
10. *The War of the Worlds;* Sir Cedric Hardwicke

QUIZ 51

1. A nervous soldier shot him accidentally
2. Robert Wise
3. Gort
4. 1951; 20th Century-Fox
5. Harry Bates; *Farewell to the Master*
6. A device for studying life on other planets
7. Washington, D.C.
8. Michael Rennie, Billy Gray, and Sam Jaffe
9. Join him and his people in peace, or face self-obliteration
10. "Klaatu Borada Nikto"

QUIZ 52

1. *Twenty Million Miles to Earth*
2. *Robot Monster*
3. Chapter nine of serial, *Exploits of Elaine*
4. *A Trip to the Moon*
5. *The Great Bet*
6. *The Diamond*
7. *Dr. Cyclops*
8. *2001: A Space Odyssey*
9. *The Lost World* (1925)
10. *The Beast of Hollow Mountain*

QUIZ 53

1. *The Day the Earth Stood Still*
2. *Bug*
3. *The Omega Man*
4. *Embryo*
5. *Futureworld*
6. *Logan's Run*
7. *At the Earth's Core*
8. *Who*
9. *The Terminal Man*
10. *Solaris*

QUIZ 54

1. Walter Hoffman
2. Byron Haskin
3. Sergie Eisenstein
4. Al Nozaki
5. Paul Frees
6. Barre Lyndon
7. Alfred Hitchcock
8. Edith Head
9. George Pal
10. 1953; Paramount

QUIZ 55

1. Pluto, Mars, Saturn, Neptune, Uranus, Jupiter, Mercury, and Earth
2. Canadian Meteorological Research Council
3. Their planet was dying, and there were no other habitable planets in the Solar System
4. Los Angeles City Hall
5. No effect
6. Les Tremayne
7. An invisible energy blister
8. In a farmhouse destroyed by a Martian landing cylinder
9. Linda Rosa
10. By Earth-bound bacteria which infect their systems

QUIZ 56

1. *Seven Days to Noon*
2. *Day the World Ended*
3. *For the Mastery of the World*
4. *The Last Woman on Earth*
5. *Lost City of the Jungle*
6. *On the Beach*
7. *Five*
8. *The Day the Earth Caught Fire*
9. *Captive Women*
10. *Teenage Cavemen*

QUIZ 57

1. g
2. j
3. a
4. e
5. b
6. c
7. d
8. f
9. i
10. h

QUIZ 58

1. Lalo Schifren
2. He stopped taking his daily dose of drugs
3. George Lucas and Walter Murch
4. LUH (played by Maggie McOmie)
5. Robert Duvall
6. In a glass booth with a single picture of Christ
7. By name tags with their numbers on them
8. Johnny Weismuller, Jr., and Robert Feero
9. The funds allotted for his pursuit have been expended
10. Francis Ford Coppola; 1971

QUIZ 59

1. *Deluge*
2. *Crack in the World*
3. *The End of the World*
4. *The Day the Sky Exploded*
5. *Once in a New Moon*
6. *The Ultimate Warrior*
7. *Voyage to the Bottom of the Sea*
8. *No Blade of Grass*
9. *Chosen Survivors*
10. *The Night the World Exploded*

QUIZ 60

1. f
2. a
3. h
4. c
5. d
6. b
7. e
8. g
9. j
10. i

QUIZ 61

1. Michael Crichton
2. Project Wildfire
3. Their entire blood supply becomes instantly clogged
4. Dr. Jeremy Stone, Dr. Charles Dutton, Dr. Mark Hall, Dr. Ruth Leavitt, and Dr. Robertson
5. Piedmont, New Mexico
6. Douglas Trumbull and James Shourt
7. The installation will self-destruct with a nuclear device
8. The fifth level
9. 1971; Universal
10. By satellite

QUIZ 62

1. *Voyage to the Bottom of the Sea*
2. *The Neptune Factor—An Undersea Odyssey*
3. *Atragon*
4. *City Beneath the Sea*
5. *Wargods of the Deep*
6. *Latitude Zero*
7. *Beast from 20,000 Fathoms*
8. *The Underwater City*
9. *The Incredible Petrified World*
10. *Captain Nemo and the Underwater City*

QUIZ 63

1. f
2. i
3. a
4. h
5. b
6. c
7. d
8. e
9. j
10. g

QUIZ 64

1. Robert Heinlein (*Rocketship Galileo*)
2. Brown, the original radio-radar operator, was stricken by an appendicitis attack
3. Warren Anderson and Tom Bowers, respectively
4. George Pal
5. *The Luna*
6. Irving Pichel
7. To survey the moon as a military missile-launching base
8. 1950
9. Four: Jim Barnes, General Thayer, Dr. Cargraves, and Sweeney
10. A saboteur is at work to delay their launch

QUIZ 65

1. *Twenty Million Miles to Earth*
2. *The Giant Claw*
3. *The Crawling Eye*
4. *The Cosmic Monsters*
5. *The Beast With a Million Eyes*
6. *The Blob*
7. *Atomic Submarine*
8. *It Conquered the World*
9. *The Day of the Triffids*
10. *Son of Blob*

QUIZ 66

1. h
2. a
3. j
4. i
5. b
6. c
7. d
8. e
9. f
10. g

QUIZ 67

1. *Blue Book* magazine in 1932
2. Bellus and Zyra
3. Cecil B. deMille who decided to do *Cleopatra* instead
4. Dr. Bronson
5. Nineteen
6. Bellus
7. George Pal
8. He is the multimillionaire who paid for the *Ark*
9. At one P.M. on July 12
10. Forty

QUIZ 68

1. *The Fantastic Journey*
2. *The Adventures of Superman*
3. *Gemini Man*
4. *The Six-Million Dollar Man*
5. *Dr. Who*
6. *Kolchak*
7. *The Atom Squad*
8. *Captain Video and the Video Rangers*
9. *Commando Cody*
10. *The Invaders*

QUIZ 69

1. b
2. f
3. i
4. a
5. h
6. j
7. c
8. g
9. d
10. e

QUIZ 70

1. Kirk Douglas and Peter Lorre, respectively
2. Nuclear power
3. 1954
4. James Mason
5. Richard Fleischer
6. Vulcania
7. John Hench and Josh Meador
8. A giant squid
9. Paul Smith
10. His personal organ

QUIZ 71

1. *Dimension X*, later known as *X Minus One*
2. *Exploring the Unknown*
3. *Flash Gordon*
4. *The Green Hornet*
5. *Latitude Zero*
6. *Buck Rogers*
7. *The Mercury Theatre on the Air*—"The War of the Worlds" episode
8. *Peter Quill*
9. *Superman*
10. *Two Thousand Plus*

QUIZ 72

1. Astronomer
2. Doctor
3. Brain surgeon
4. Professor
5. Inventor
6. Newspaper columnist, his real-life profession
7. Bum
8. A beautiful costumer of New You, a cosmetic surgery boutique
9. Inventor
10. Businessman

QUIZ 73

1. 2293
2. The idol worshipped by the Exterminators
3. John Boorman
4. Zed is mentally and physically superior to the Vortex people
5. Sean Connery and Charlotte Rampling, respectively
6. A trance-like state known as "second-level meditation"
7. The Vortex and the Outlands
8. He shoots the man operating the idol
9. The Eternals, the Renegades, and the Apathetics
10. Geoffrey Unsworth

QUIZ 74

1. *Armageddon 2419 A.D.*
2. 500 years
3. Nirvano gas
4. Buster Crabbe
5. Killer Kane
6. Zapguns, paralyzing pistols, degravity belts, and invisible rays
7. Philip Nowlan
8. When a Filament Ray Helmet is used against him by Killer Kane
9. Dr. Huer
10. The Zuggs; Saturn

QUIZ 75

1. e
2. a
3. i
4. g
5. j
6. h
7. f
8. b
9. c
10. d

QUIZ 76

1. France and Czechoslovakia
2. Ygam
3. The small race of humans who are in conflict with the Draags
4. Rene LaLoux
5. Tiwa
6. *Oms En Sevie* by Stefan Wiel
7. Thirty-nine feet
8. By grouping themselves into large numbers and overwhelming the Draags
9. Roland Topor
10. Red

QUIZ 77

1. *The Mysterians*
2. *Gog*
3. *Tobar the Great*
4. *The Invisible Boy*
5. *Target Earth!*
6. *The Perfect Woman*
7. *Robot Monster*
8. *The Creation of the Humanoids*
9. *King Kong Escapes*
10. *The Colossus of New York*

QUIZ 78

1. b
2. g
3. j
4. e
5. f
6. a
7. c
8. d
9. i
10. h

QUIZ 79

1. To allow for expansion of the enormous human population
2. Huey and Dewey
3. American Airlines Space Freighters
4. Douglas Trumbull
5. The Conservationists' pledge
6. The *Valley Forge*
7. Saturn
8. Joan Baez
9. Huey
10. The forest

QUIZ 80

1. *Land of the Giants*
2. *Land of the Lost*
3. *Lost in Space*
4. *The Lost Saucer*
5. *My Favorite Martian*
6. *Out There*
7. *Planet of the Apes*
8. *Rod Brown of the Rocket Rangers*
9. *Science Fiction Theatre*
10. *Space: 1999*

QUIZ 81

1. Thermostellar bomb # 19
2. Dan O'Bannon, Brian Navelle, and Carl Kuniholm, respectively
3. U.S.C.
4. To drop bombs on suns that are about to go nova
5. Commander Powell
6. A phenomenological argument
7. He designed the *Dark Star*
8. John Carpenter
9. A rubber mouse
10. Dan O'Bannon

QUIZ 82

1. *The Immortal*
2. *Daughter of the Mind*
3. *The Challenge*
4. *The Love War*
5. *The Night Slavers*
6. *The Man Who Wanted to Live Forever*
7. *The Deadly Dream*
8. *The Last Child*
9. *Madam Sin*
10. *Rachel, Sweet Rachel*

QUIZ 83

1. *Future Cop*
2. *The Last Dinosaur*
3. *Quark*
4. *The Day After Tomorrow*
5. *The Man from Atlantis*
6. *The Savage Bees*
7. *Where Have All the People Gone?*
8. *Strange New World*
9. *Time Travelers*
10. *The UFO Incident*

QUIZ 84

1. a
2. e
3. b
4. f
5. d
6. i
7. g
8. h
9. c
10. j

QUIZ 85

1. 2024
2. Roverpacks
3. Blood
4. Topeka, Kansas
5. Tim McIntire
6. Don Johnson
7. Ray Boyle
8. The Nebula
9. Jason Robards
10. L. Q. Jones

QUIZ 86

1. *King of the Rocket Men*
2. *The Undersea Kingdom*
3. *The Phantom Empire*
4. *The Master Mystery* (with Harry Houdini, 1918)
5. *The Spider Returns*
6. *The Fighting Devil Dogs*
7. *Hop Harrigan*
8. *Radar Patrol vs. Spy King*
9. *Superman* (1948)
10. *The Adventures of Captain Marvel*

QUIZ 87

1. h
2. f
3. c
4. e
5. d
6. i
7. g
8. j
9. a
10. b

QUIZ 88

1. Blackwolf
2. *Fritz the Cat, Heavy Traffic,* and *Coonskin*
3. Elinor
4. Montaga
5. Ted C. Bemiller
6. A film projector
7. Andrew Belling
8. A library of Nazi propaganda films
9. Scorch I
10. Avatar

QUIZ 89

1. g
2. h
3. j
4. c
5. f
6. e
7. a
8. i
9. b
10. d

QUIZ 90

1. f
2. a
3. d
4. g
5. h
6. b
7. c
8. j
9. e
10. i

QUIZ 91

1. Delos
2. John Blane
3. Michael Crichton
4. Peter Martin
5. 1973; M.G.M.
6. Yul Brynner
7. After they sleep with two robot-prostitutes
8. Rome, The Middle Ages, and the West
9. John Blane
10. Richard Benjamin and James Brolin, respectively

QUIZ 92

1. *The Alligator People*
2. *The Amazing Colossal Man*
3. *War of the Colossal Beast*
4. *Attack of the Fifty-Foot Woman*
5. *Return of the Fly*
6. *The Hideous Sun Demon*
7. *The Creeping Unknown*
8. *The Indestructible Man*
9. *Creature with the Atom Brain*
10. *The Manster*

QUIZ 93

1. The Twenty-first Century
2. The Corporations
3. Norman Jewison
4. The Energy Corporation
5. Five skaters, three bikers, and two catchers
6. Cletus
7. He is becoming too popular
8. James Caan
9. Zero
10. *Roller Ball Murder* (by William Harrison)

QUIZ 94

1. i
2. j
3. f
4. h
5. c
6. e
7. d
8. b
9. g
10. a

QUIZ 95

1. *The Thing*
2. *This Island Earth*
3. *The Day the Earth Stood Still*
4. *Cosmic Man*
5. *The Astounding She-Monster*
6. *Plan Nine from Outer Space*
7. *Teenagers from Outer Space*
8. *Brain from Planet Arous*
9. *Phantom from Space*
10. *The Space Children*

QUIZ 96

1. *Killers from Space*
2. *The Man from Planet X*
3. *The Twonky*
4. *Flame Barrier*
5. *The 27th Day*
6. *The Monolith Monsters*
7. *Enemy from Space*
8. *Terror from the Year 5000*
9. *War of the Satellites*
10. *Invaders from Mars*

QUIZ 97

1. A drunk in an amusement park
2. Thomas Jerome Newton
3. "Hello, MaryLou," "Rhumba Boogie," "A Fool Such as I," "Blue Bayou," and "Silent Night"
4. Paul Mayersberg
5. Anthea
6. John Phillips
7. Nicholas Roeg
8. His contact lenses become stuck to his eyes
9. Oliver Farnsworth (played by Buck Henry)
10. *The Third Man*

QUIZ 98

1. f
2. b
3. e
4. i
5. a
6. d
7. j
8. c
9. g
10. h

QUIZ 99

1. Everytown
2. William Cameron Menzies
3. Ned Mann
4. World War Two, and the development of the A-bomb
5. John Cable
6. H. G. Wells
7. By a society of super-scientific minds
8. Wings Over the World, a Basra-based organization of law and sanity
9. Passworthy's son and John Cable's daughter
10. 1936; Great Britain

QUIZ 100

1. Zahgons
2. Indio, California
3. Gog and Magog
4. Metaluna
5. Wade Powell
6. Zoomite for his Dooflebox
7. Mona
8. X7
9. Velona
10. Chani
11. Eddie Parker

PHOTO QUIZ

1. *Revenge of the Creature* and *The Creature Walks Among Us* (original—*The Creature From the Black Lagoon*)
2. Plague wars
3. The Martians
4. Kirk Alyn
5. *Panic in the Year Zero*
6. Esmeralda
7. *Futureworld*
8. Exterminators
9. Mars
10. *Tarantula*
11. She cut off his drug supply and he fell in love with her (from *THX-1138*)
12. 2250 (from *Forbidden Planet*)
13. Kim Hunter, Charlton Heston, and Linda Harrison; *Planet of the Apes*
14. A bleak landscape devastated by atomic warfare and populated by mutants (from *Rocketship XM*)
15. *Planet of the Vampires*
16. *The Shrinking Man* by Richard Matheson
17. Ron Burke
18. Henry
19. *Soylent Green*
20. That she has been transformed by Martian invaders (from *Invaders from Mars*)
21. Ray Harryhausen with Russ Kelley
22. Four
23. Roger Corman
24. Giant ants

154